Discovering the United States

Massachusetts

BY LAURA STICKNEY

Kids Core
An Imprint of Abdo Publishing
abdobooks.com

abdobooks.com

Published by Abdo Publishing, a division of ABDO, PO Box 398166, Minneapolis, Minnesota 55439. Copyright © 2025 by Abdo Consulting Group, Inc. International copyrights reserved in all countries. No part of this book may be reproduced in any form without written permission from the publisher. Kids Core™ is a trademark and logo of Abdo Publishing.

Printed in the United States of America, North Mankato, Minnesota.
052024
092024

THIS BOOK CONTAINS RECYCLED MATERIALS

Cover Photo: Sean Pavone/Shutterstock Images
Interior Photos: Ed Vebell/Archive Photos/Getty Images, 4–5; LnP Images/Shutterstock Images, 7; Shutterstock Images, 8 (top left), 8 (bottom right), 26, 28 (right); iStockphoto, 8 (top right); Adriana Iacob/Shutterstock Images, 8 (bottom left); Denis Tangney Jr./iStockphoto, 10; Erin Clark/Boston Globe/Getty Images, 12–13; David L. Ryan/Boston Globe/Getty Images, 15; Mariia Kozub/iStockphoto, 16; Billie Weiss/Boston Red Sox/Getty Images Sport/Getty Images, 17; Zack Frank/Shutterstock Images, 20–21, 29 (bottom); Ilaria Perriu/Shutterstock Images, 23; Goss Images/Alamy, 24; Red Line Editorial, 28 (left), 29 (top)

Editor: Christa Kelly
Series Designer: Katharine Hale

Library of Congress Control Number: 2023949385

Publisher's Cataloging-in-Publication Data

Names: Stickney, Laura, author.
Title: Massachusetts / by Laura Stickney
Description: Minneapolis, Minnesota: Abdo Publishing, 2025 | Series: Discovering the United States | Includes online resources and index.
Identifiers: ISBN 9781098293918 (lib. bdg.) | ISBN 9798384913184 (ebook)
Subjects: LCSH: U.S. states--Juvenile literature. | Massachusetts--History--Juvenile literature. | Northeastern States--Juvenile literature. | Physical geography--United States--Juvenile literature.
Classification: DDC 973--dc23

All population data taken from:
"Estimates of Population by Sex, Race, and Hispanic Origin: April 1, 2020 to July 1, 2022." *US Census Bureau, Population Division*, June 2023, census.gov.

CONTENTS

CHAPTER 1
The Boston Tea Party 4

CHAPTER 2
The People of Massachusetts 12

CHAPTER 3
Places in Massachusetts 20

State Map 28
Glossary 30
Online Resources 31
Learn More 31
Index 32
About the Author 32

The men who dumped tea into Boston Harbor in December 1773 called themselves the Sons of Liberty. They dressed as American Indians to identify themselves as American, not British.

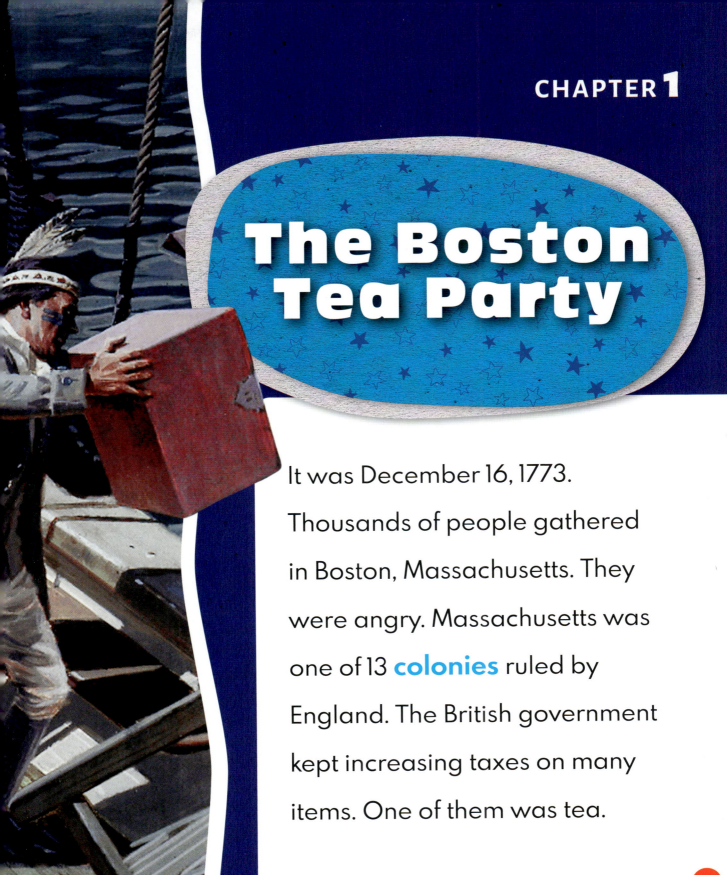

CHAPTER 1

The Boston Tea Party

It was December 16, 1773. Thousands of people gathered in Boston, Massachusetts. They were angry. Massachusetts was one of 13 **colonies** ruled by England. The British government kept increasing taxes on many items. One of them was tea.

But the colonists did not get to pick who represented them in the government. They thought they should not be taxed without a say in how they were ruled.

That night, the group marched to Griffin's Wharf. Ships carrying tea were docked there. The colonists **raided** the ships. They smashed open 340 tea chests. They dumped them overboard. The protesters destroyed more than 92,000 pounds (42,000 kg) of tea.

This event became known as the Boston Tea Party. It was the colonists' first big protest against the British. It helped spark the Revolutionary War (1775–1783). More than 300 years later, the Boston Tea Party remains an important moment in Massachusetts's history.

The Boston Tea Party Ships & Museum is a popular tourist spot in Boston Harbor.

Land and Wildlife

Massachusetts is in the Northeast region of the United States. The state's northern edge borders both New Hampshire and Vermont.

Massachusetts Facts

DATE OF STATEHOOD
February 6, 1788

CAPITAL
Boston

POPULATION
6,981,974

AREA
10,554 square miles
(27,335 sq km)

STATE BIRD

Black-capped chickadee

STATE TREE

American elm

STATE FLOWER
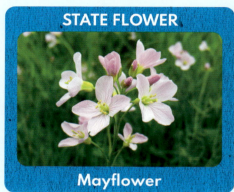
Mayflower

STATE FISH
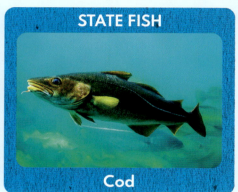
Cod

Each US state has a different population, size, and capital city. States also have state symbols.

To the west is New York. To the south are Connecticut, Rhode Island, and the Atlantic Ocean. The ocean also borders Massachusetts to the east.

The state is covered in forests, plains, and rocky beaches. The land is mostly flat, but there are some hills and mountains in western Massachusetts. This area includes the Berkshire Hills and Mount Greylock, the state's highest point. The Housatonic River cuts through the hills.

Massachusetts has many **harbors** and **bays**. Islands lie off its southeastern coast.

The Bay State

Massachusetts is nicknamed the Bay State. This is because many bays lie along its coastline. Massachusetts Bay is along the state's northern coast. Inside it lies Boston Bay. Buzzards Bay and Cape Cod Bay are located along the state's southeastern coast.

Many people visit Massachusetts in the fall to see the bright colors of the leaves.

Massachusetts is also home to plants such as American elm trees. Many animals, including chickadees, also call the state home.

Weather

Massachusetts has warm summers and cold winters. In winter, temperatures are warmer near the eastern coast and colder in the west. Spring and summer bring rain. Fall brings brightly colored leaves to the trees.

Big storms are common during colder months. People call these storms nor'easters. They bring rain and wind. If it is cold enough, they can also bring heavy snow.

Explore Online

Visit the website below. Does it give any new information about Massachusetts that wasn't in Chapter One?

Massachusetts

abdocorelibrary.com/discovering-massachusetts

A woman celebrates the 2021 Indigenous People's Day in Newton, Massachusetts. The holiday comes each year on the second Monday in October.

CHAPTER 2

The People of Massachusetts

American Indians have lived in Massachusetts for more than 12,000 years. They formed nations. These nations include the Massachusett and Wampanoag. The people of these nations hunted and fished. They grew corn and squash.

In the 1600s, white English settlers arrived in Massachusetts. They brought diseases that American Indians were not **immune** to. Because of this, many American Indians died. Many others were driven off their land through a series of wars in the 1600s and 1700s.

In the 1800s, many people came to Massachusetts from Canada and Europe. In the 1950s, many Black Americans moved to Massachusetts. Most came from southern states.

About 70 percent of people in Massachusetts are white. More than 13 percent are Hispanic or Latino. About 10 percent of the people are Black. Asian Americans make up 8 percent of the population. American Indians make up 0.5 percent.

Visitors to Plimoth Patuxet Museums in Plymouth, Massachusetts, can see a recreation of a settlers' village from 1627.

Culture

Food is an important part of Massachusetts's culture. Many people in the state fish, so seafood such as lobster and cod is common. One popular dish is clam chowder. It is a soup made with clams and potatoes in a creamy broth.

The Boston cream pie was invented at one of the city's hotels in 1856.

Boston cream pie is popular. It has yellow cake with vanilla custard and chocolate frosting.

Sports are important to the state's culture. Boston is home to Fenway Park, where the Red Sox baseball team plays. The city is also the site of the Boston Marathon. This 26.2-mile (42-km) race happens every year. Thousands of runners visit Massachusetts to compete in it.

Built in 1912, Fenway Park is the oldest stadium in Major League Baseball.

Working in Massachusetts

Fishing is an important **industry** on the coast of Massachusetts. In 2019, Massachusetts was one of the nation's top seafood producers.

Fishers catch and sell scallops, lobsters, and oysters. Farmers in the state grow cranberries.

Massachusetts also has many technology companies. Boston Scientific focuses on medical technology. Education is another important industry. The state has many well-known colleges, including Harvard University and Massachusetts Institute of Technology.

Famous Writers

Many famous writers lived in Massachusetts. Poet Emily Dickinson lived in Amherst. Nathaniel Hawthorne and Louisa May Alcott both lived in Concord. Hawthorne wrote novels and short stories. Alcott wrote *Little Women*, which is about four sisters growing up in the 1800s. Today, people can visit these writers' homes.

Dan McKiernan leads the state's Division of Marine Fisheries. This organization manages the state's ocean fish. He said:

> A lot of communities take pride in their waterfront, and in the fact that they are a seafood producing town. And it's a . . . source of income for these ports.

Source: Julia Wells. "State Makes Millions More Available in Aid for Fishing Industry." *Vineyard Gazette*, 25 July 2021, vineyardgazette.com. Accessed 30 Aug. 2023.

What's the Big Idea?

Read this quote carefully. What is its main idea? Explain how the main idea is supported by details.

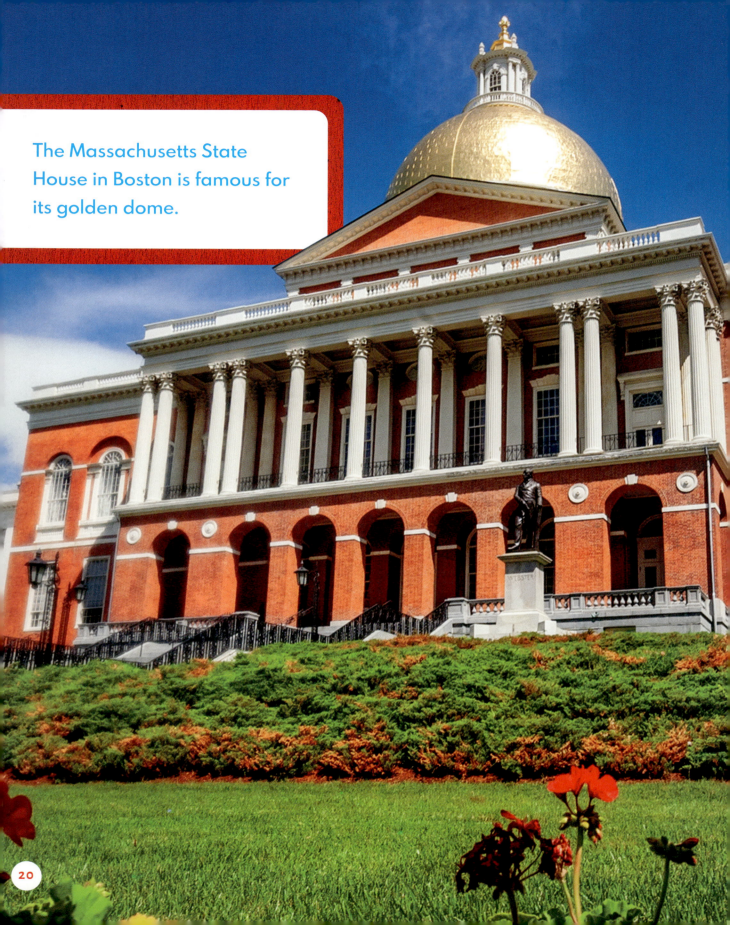

The Massachusetts State House in Boston is famous for its golden dome.

CHAPTER 3

Places in Massachusetts

The capital of Massachusetts is Boston. It is on the state's eastern coast. Boston is the largest city in the state by population.

The state's second-largest city is Worcester. It is in central Massachusetts. It is home to many colleges and museums.

Springfield is in the southwest. This historic city is where children's author Dr. Seuss was born. People can learn about him at the city's Dr. Seuss museum.

Massachusetts is home to three American Indian reservations. One is Nipmuc. The other two are Wampanoag.

Parks and Nature

Massachusetts has many important national sites. Cape Cod National Seashore covers 40 miles (64 km) of land along eastern Cape Cod. People can visit the seashore's lighthouses and beaches. Boston Harbor Islands is another nationally protected site. It has 34 islands and **peninsulas**.

Visitors can often see whales off the shores of Cape Cod.

Massachusetts also has 48 state parks. One popular state park is Bash Bish Falls. It's home to the state's highest waterfall.

Landmarks

Many Massachusetts landmarks **commemorate** the Revolutionary War. One such landmark is the Freedom Trail. This is a 2.5-mile (4-km) line on the ground in Boston.

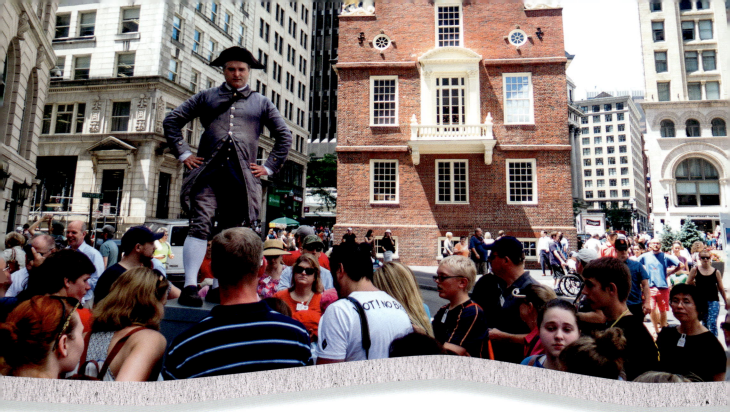

Tour guides wearing colonial-era costumes are often seen in Boston, especially along the Freedom Trail.

It leads visitors to 16 historical sites. One of the stops is Boston Common, the country's oldest public park. Bunker Hill Monument is another site on the trail. This monument marks a battlefield.

The Boston Tea Party Ships & Museum is also in Boston. Visitors can learn about the Boston Tea Party and throw fake tea into the harbor.

In nearby Concord, tourists can visit Minute Man National Historical Park. The park marks the first battlefields of the Revolutionary War.

The town of Salem is another Massachusetts historic site. In 1692, more than 200 people in Salem were accused of witchcraft. Twenty-five of the accused were killed. People can learn about the trials at the Salem Witch Museum.

Whaling

In the mid-1800s, fishers in Massachusetts hunted whales. They used the whales' body parts to make products. Whale oil was especially valuable. It could be turned into candles, cleaning chemicals, and more. Today, commercial whaling is illegal in the United States.

The Massachusetts state flag includes a Latin phrase. It translates to "By the sword we seek peace, but peace only under liberty."

The islands of Nantucket and Martha's Vineyard are popular tourist sites. They are known for their scenic towns and beaches. Many people visit the islands during the summer.

Massachusetts has a mixture of landscapes, historical sites, and cultures. People can relive the past on the Freedom Trail. They can try popular foods. They can see the state's scenic coastlines. Massachusetts is full of places to explore.

Further Evidence

Look at the website below, which contains a list of Freedom Trail sites. Does it give any new evidence to support Chapter Three?

Freedom Trail Historic Sites

abdocorelibrary.com/discovering-massachusetts

State Map

KEY

 Capital Park

 City or town Point of interest

Bash Bish Falls State Park

Massachusetts: The Bay State

Massachusetts State House

Glossary

bay
a small body of water connected to an ocean or lake

colony
an area that is controlled by another country

commemorate
to remember and honor

harbor
an area of deep water near the shore where ships can dock

immune
when a person's body knows how to fight a disease

industry
a group of businesses that serve similar purposes

peninsulas
areas of land surrounded by water on three sides

raided
broke into or attacked a place and stole from it

Online Resources

To learn more about Massachusetts, visit our free resource websites below.

Visit **abdocorelibrary.com** or scan this QR code for free Common Core resources for teachers and students, including vetted activities, multimedia, and booklinks, for deeper subject comprehension.

Visit **abdobooklinks.com** or scan this QR code for free additional online weblinks for further learning. These links are routinely monitored and updated to provide the most current information available.

Learn More

Berne, Emma Carlson. *The History of the American Revolution*. Rockridge, 2021.

Messner, Kate. *The Mayflower*. Random House, 2020.

Murray, Julie. *Massachusetts*. Abdo, 2020.

Index

Bash Bish Falls, 23
bays, 9
Boston, 5, 21, 24
Boston Tea Party, 6, 24

Cape Cod, 22

fishing, 17–18, 19
food, 15–18, 27
Freedom Trail, 23–24, 27

Harvard University, 18

immigrants, 14

Massachusett peoples, 13
Massachusetts Institute of Technology (MIT), 18
McKiernan, Dan, 19
Mount Greylock, 9

Nipmuc peoples, 22

Salem, 25
Springfield, 22
state symbols, 8, 10

Wampanoag peoples, 13, 22
Worcester, 21

About the Author

Laura Stickney is a writer, editor, and artist from the Twin Cities area in Minnesota. She visited Massachusetts as a teen. Her favorite thing to do there was walk the Freedom Trail.